Waiting...

Devotions for the Journey

Dr. Lee Ann B. Marino, Ph.D., D.Min., D.D.

Waiting...
Devotions for the Journey

Dr. Lee Ann B. Marino, Ph.D., D.Min., D.D.

Published by:

Remnant Words

(An imprint of the Righteous Pen Publications Group)

www.righteouspenpublications.com

All rights reserved. Except as permitted under the U.S. Copyright Act of 1976, no part of this book may be reproduced, distributed, or transmitted in any form or by any means, electronic or mechanical, or saved in any information storage and retrieval system without written permission from the author.

Unless otherwise indicated, all Scripture quotations are taken from **the Amplified® Bible, Classic Edition** Copyright © 1954, 1958, 1962, 1964, 1965, 1987 by The Lockman Foundation. Used by permission." (www.Lockman.org)

Book classification: 1. Books > Religion & Spirituality > Worship & Devotion > Devotionals.

Copyright © 2020 by Lee Ann B. Marino.

ISBN: 1-940197-62-7
13-Digit: 978-1-940197-62-3

Printed in the United States of America.

Waiting for a train to go or a bus to come,
or a plane to go or the mail to come,
or the rain to go or the phone to ring,
or the snow to snow or waiting around
for a Yes or No
or waiting for their hair to grow.

Everyone is just waiting.

Waiting for the fish to bite
or waiting for wind to fly a kite
or waiting around for Friday night
or waiting, perhaps, for their Uncle Jake
or a pot to boil, or a Better Break
or a string of pearls, or a pair of pants
or a wig with curls, or Another Chance.

Everyone is just waiting.

(Dr Seuss, "The Waiting Place")

– Table of Contents –

	Word From the Author	i
1	I am Not Fine Today	1
2	Under Pressure	3
3	Help My Unbelief	5
4	Just Another Day in Paradise	7
5	Much Ado About Waiting	9
6	There are No Secrets	11
7	All We Need is Just a Little Patience	13
8	I Won't Back Down	15
9	Unless a Grain of Wheat Falls	17
10	Unspoken Conversations	19
11	One More Night	21
12	Suffering	23
13	Learning to be Uncomfortable	25
14	All Eyes on You	27
15	Exposed!	29
16	It is What it is	31
17	The Treasures of Darkness	33
18	Unsatisfactory Answers	35
19	Great Expectations	37
20	All That You Can't Leave Behind	39
21	The Fullness of Time	41
22	Holy Ground	43
23	Hope	45
24	Paradigm Shift	47
25	Veiled in Silence	49
26	The Sign of Jonah	51
27	New Wine	53
28	The Waiting is the Hardest Part	55
	Afterword: When God Gives the Darkness	57
	References	59
	Other Books of Interest by The Author	61
	About the Author	63

– WORD FROM THE AUTHOR –

January 4, 2019 was the day that changed my entire life. I arose very early in the morning to take my husband of 11 years to UNC Chapel Hill to discover he had Stage IV metastatic liver cancer and advanced cirrhosis. He was given anywhere between two and 11 months left to live, with the reality being he would, most likely, live closer to two months than 11. It was an announcement that was both shocking and scary, as I began the walk with him toward the end of his life. In what would wind up being only 22 days from diagnosis to death, I found myself doing everything I knew to do to care for him and process my own shock and dismay as I realized this most unfortunate situation would bring a difficult and journeying end to a complicated and difficult marriage. I went through my own feelings, my own resolutions, my own thoughts and ideas, to come out and discover I was in a situation that involved a lot of waiting. I knew what was coming. I didn't know how imminent it was, but I knew I was waiting for something to come that would change my life.

While sitting in appointments that always led to bad news, dreading the night hours because I was afraid something would happen while I was asleep, and not knowing what to do next, I got the idea for a devotional that was all about waiting. We seldom wait well, especially when the waiting process is hard. We grow impatient, frustrated, and despondent with the process. God can feel far away while we wait and even farther away when the end of the wait is hard to the point of total change and transformation. While we wait, we try to find ways to avoid the wait, deny the wait, or find our way out of it, but seldom, if ever, do we step back and examine the process of the wait. We hope to get from point A to point B as quickly as possible, with no stops involved.

Nobody likes to wait...so we do it badly. We miss the point of the wait. Waiting, however, is the very point and process of transformation we claim to seek. The changes we experience while waiting aren't always positive, great, uplifting, or encouraging. Change, in fact, can often feel like the opposite of the things we hear it to be. There's a reason we avoid it; there's a reason we avoid the waiting we dread; we hope to skip and move on to better days. The problem with this is that we can't get to what we seek if we don't take the bad with the good, and if we aren't willing to sit through our own personal experiences that leave us feeling less than fantastic.

Here, I reflect on my own experiences with waiting and offer insights therein; the depth, the dark, the difficult, and ultimately, the light that shines there like it does nowhere else. I'm not just sharing ideas, but the revelation on essential concepts about waiting and all of us can learn from such periods in time. For 28 days, we delve into the difficulties, the wisdom, and the insights of spiritual darkness, those times while we wait for night to end and light to come. In these places and times, we hear God calling us: not just to change, but to draw to Him deeper, as we learn to accept the good and the bad alike. Here, we see the ultimate hope and transformation He works to do within each of us. Hard and pressing, it is through these difficult times we find the power of God released within us so we, too, can find His light and then carry it to others.

This is my "waiting journal," of sorts: The outcome of a personal journey that I pray, can bring light to the darkness that is waiting, hope in places of tumult and change, and ultimately, the encouragement that even though you might not see it right now, God is still working within you.

− 1 −
I AM NOT FINE TODAY

YES, THOUGH I WALK THROUGH THE [DEEP, SUNLESS] VALLEY OF THE SHADOW OF DEATH, I WILL FEAR OR DREAD NO EVIL, FOR YOU ARE WITH ME; YOUR ROD [TO PROTECT] AND YOUR STAFF [TO GUIDE], THEY COMFORT ME.
(PSALM 23:4)

- Reading: Psalm 42:1-11
- Insight: If you are waiting, you are changing.

When we wait, we have an overwhelming sense of anticipation. This strange, sometimes unsettling sense leaves us hyper-aware of our existing situations. Where we might have been content and peaceful to live our lives and mind our own business, our world is suddenly disrupted. No longer are we fine, content, even happy to remain where we are. We're handling something that is leading to something else. At points, it can't come fast enough. We search; we strive for the answers to our situation, until we come to the point where we recognize there isn't anything we can to do hasten things along. All we can do is wait and see...and be awkward in the meantime.

One of the reasons we often hate to wait is because it promotes in us this sense of awkward uneasiness that doesn't just make us uncomfortable in our interior lives. When we are waiting, it makes other people uncomfortable, as well. The things we used to have in common we have either lost or don't feel as central or important anymore. They might still be there, but the perspective of things is changing. Others might not know what to talk about. We might view their behavior differently or feel different about them, too. All those things that plague their thoughts, their preoccupations, and their idiosyncrasies suddenly seem...trite.

So when asked, "How are you?" The answer may not, in actuality, be "fine." "Fine" might be the word that comes out of our mouths, but there is nothing "fine" about us. We are waiting, transitioning, changing to become something other than we are right now. It's perfectly normal, acceptable, and real to not feel all right when a transition is in process. If you're not feeling all right, own it. Recognize it. You won't ever move through the period successfully, and with needed closure, if you don't. Instead of letting others dictate how you feel or think, own and embrace how you are feeling, right now, as you wait.

It is perfectly honest and acceptable to admit that those you've been around, close to, in contact with, or connected to for some time might not understand, nor accept, that you aren't "fine" anymore. You don't have to lie or pretend like things aren't happening to satisfy other people who don't easily understand what you're experiencing. Trust those you speak with and be honest about how you are feeling. You will come to find, perhaps even by accident, many important life lessons and realities come to light as you wait...and hope...and prepare.

- 2 -
UNDER PRESSURE

*IF YOU FAINT IN THE DAY OF ADVERSITY,
YOUR STRENGTH IS SMALL.
(PROVERBS 24:10)*

- <u>Reading</u>: 2 Corinthians 10:1-7
- <u>Insight</u>: Pressure births spiritual purpose.

Whenever we take a long look at leaders in Scripture, we often extol specific positive characteristics in those individuals who wrestled with the challenges of leadership. Abraham was bold. Moses was strong. David was noble. The Apostle Peter was committed. The Apostle Paul was devoted. These different characteristics of leadership sound great and perfect, complete in their own right. It's easy for us to look at them and think they didn't experience the challenges we do as part of everyday living. In between their boldness, strength, nobility, commitment, and devotion, we think they were restful and peaceful, and waited with perfect anticipation of things to come.

Truth be told, all these leaders experienced a powerful sting of waiting: pressure. They felt their own pressures as they saw things changing and transforming around them. Would they be able to keep up? Were all these movements heading in a right direction? Was there a place for them as things would move toward a place of change? Then there was the bigger question they all asked God at some point in time: How in the world do I handle all these people while I wait?

Waiting brings with it a sense of pressure: pressure from within, pressure from circumstances, and pressure from those around us. We always want to know why, when, and how, but waiting doesn't answer us. The pressure is intense as we are moved, pressed, and pushed to move through our waiting period into something else.

In our pressing, crushing, and pushing periods, we see something deeper come forth from our difficult situations. Though certainly not perfect people, Abraham, Moses, David, Peter, and Paul were all good leaders because they learned how to handle themselves under pressure, in the most difficult and trying circumstances they had to face. It doesn't mean they never lost their tempers or sight of what God might have had in store, because it's obvious they all had times where they lost their cool and asked the bigger life questions as necessary. They found the answers they sought, however, as they allowed the process of waiting to take its form and followed as God led, day in and day out.

I've been asked, why does God often wait to move until the absolute last minute? It's because God knows the importance of the waiting process, and He desires His people to be fruitful under pressure. We will only learn how to deal with pressure if we experience it. We experience pressure, fully, while we wait.

- 3 -
HELP MY UNBELIEF

AND JESUS SAID, [YOU SAY TO ME], IF YOU CAN DO ANYTHING? [WHY,] ALL THINGS CAN BE (ARE POSSIBLE) TO HIM WHO BELIEVES! AT ONCE THE FATHER OF THE BOY GAVE [AN EAGER, PIERCING, INARTICULATE] CRY WITH TEARS, AND HE SAID, LORD, I BELIEVE! [CONSTANTLY] HELP MY WEAKNESS OF FAITH!
(MARK 9:23-24)

- <u>Reading</u>: Hebrews 4:1-16
- <u>Insight</u>: Belief is stronger than unbelief.

The challenge of belief is seldom a matter simple as trying to reason ourselves into faith. We can read all the books, remember all the great things God has done for us, surround ourselves with the best in Christian believers, and still wrestle with uncertainty about our future. This is truer while we wait, more than at any other time in our lives. When we aren't certain as to where we are heading and feeling disconnected and distant from our past, it is no wonder that we struggle, in times of waiting, with unbelief.

    I don't believe that "unbelief" is the same thing as refusing to believe or not believing at all. If someone doesn't believe in something, there is no struggle present. When a person struggles with unbelief, it is the result of a period in life that leaves one with questions that aren't easily answered. These aren't questions we can get answers from within someone else's perspective, but ones we must ask, and discover the answers, as we walk and experience through the period of life that causes us to ask those difficult questions.

Unbelief is answered through experience; by walking with God and seeing Him come through, time and time again, in our lives. It is a condition overcome as our faith increases, trusting God for what we don't see because we know what we have seen for ourselves. Instead of relying on the word or thoughts of someone else, we can see it real, even when we don't quite understand yet just how it will manifest in our specific circumstance. Unbelief is overcome by faith, because faith inspires us to hope as we wait.

In times of waiting, we are challenged to faith as we wrestle with unbelief. As we wait, we come face-to-face with our interior lives and discussions that we often hide and cover in periods where things are good and seem balanced. When things are great, we convince ourselves our issues with fear aren't as real as they might be. We pretend our anxieties and doubts aren't there anymore. We imagine the questions we have about life and bigger realities are answered, and we are content to stay with these denials through these better times. When we wait, however, we feel and experience our unbelief as it comes to the surface. It's there, it haunts us, and we can't deny it, will it, or pretend it away.

We deal with ourselves while we wait, or we wait longer. We see what we need to change, what we need to learn, and what we need to discover. In the beauty of the wait, we experience spiritual growth. We ask the questions we need to ask, and we resolve to address and overcome the interior places within us that wrestle with unbelief.

- 4 -
JUST ANOTHER DAY IN PARADISE

MOREOVER [LET US ALSO BE FULL OF JOY NOW!] LET US EXULT AND TRIUMPH IN OUR TROUBLES AND REJOICE IN OUR SUFFERINGS, KNOWING THAT PRESSURE AND AFFLICTION AND HARDSHIP PRODUCE PATIENT AND UNSWERVING ENDURANCE. AND ENDURANCE (FORTITUDE) DEVELOPS MATURITY OF CHARACTER (APPROVED FAITH AND TRIED INTEGRITY). AND CHARACTER [OF THIS SORT] PRODUCES [THE HABIT OF] JOYFUL AND CONFIDENT HOPE OF ETERNAL SALVATION.
(ROMANS 5:3-4)

- <u>Reading</u>: James 1:1-8
- <u>Insight</u>: Spiritual growth requires difficult experiences.

Stress and waiting often go hand-in-hand. In the smaller examples of life, we often feel great stress when we are waiting for an appointment, test results, examination results, for news (whether good or bad), or just sense that something is now on the horizon. The stress we experience in the process can lead us to feel a general sense of dread, anxiety, haste, worry, or tumult, all because we confront the world of the unknown, head on. In waiting, we find ourselves at that meeting place between what we know and don't know, all rolled into one major, uncomfortable experience.

When we wait, it can feel like an exhausting, long process. Day rolls into day, all with the same feelings of stress, anxiety, and sometimes, dread. We feel that way because in not knowing, we don't know what to expect or what shall come next. Life can feel hopeless, difficult, arduous, and like a huge downer. Each day as we wait becomes just another day we wait. We wade, in an ironic "paradise" that, is, of course, the opposite of true paradise. It's a place of discomfort that has a nasty way of lingering.

It's important to remember that periods of waiting always end, often as surprising as the circumstance that started our process of waiting began. As we wait, it is most operative that we try to discern what lurks just beneath the chaos that seems to rage both within and around us. Our periods of waiting do not exist to no avail; they exist to reveal things about ourselves; our changing landscapes, our hopes and dreams, maybe even things we want to do that we'd forgotten about or didn't realize until we had to get real, in this place where we wait. Waiting periods are not the end but are promising times in life where shifting gives us the opportunity to dig deep and be honest about who we are and where we desire to go in this life.

It isn't God's desire that we go through life seeking nothing more than ease and comfort. Such is a nice idea, but we don't grow without challenge. We don't change if nothing forces us into that place of true self-examination and honesty. If you are seeking nothing but literal paradise, you will never find it. If you accept that in waiting, we often experience those genuine, sarcastic, "just another day in paradise!" periods, you will come much closer to the dimensional richness given to us in difficult times. It takes the bad as well as the good to grow into the full stature of our faith. In those turbulent, hard times, we are best able to grow closer to God.

- 5 -
MUCH ADO ABOUT WAITING

*I WAIT FOR THE LORD, I EXPECTANTLY WAIT,
AND IN HIS WORD DO I HOPE.
I AM LOOKING AND WAITING FOR THE LORD
MORE THAN WATCHMEN FOR THE MORNING,
I SAY, MORE THAN WATCHMEN FOR THE MORNING.
(PSALM 130:5-6)*

- <u>Reading</u>: Lamentations 3:1-31
- <u>Insight</u>: Complaining does not terminate waiting.

Waiting is one of those aspects of life we complain about...sometimes incessantly. When we are waiting for something, someone, or some change, everyone knows about it. We hastily, and often with great frustration, declare to others, "I'm waiting!" Maybe some part of us thinks if we spread the news, someone can do something to shorten our waiting period. Whatever our thought process, we want everyone to know we are waiting, how uncomfortable we are with the situation, and that we hope – and believe – for something better, shorter, different – to be just around the corner.

Waiting brings out the "fussing" in us; the parts of us that like to fuss, to complain, to be the center of everyone's attention because we are uncomfortable or discontented. I don't think it's a huge stretch of the imagination to acknowledge that when we are upset, we want others to acknowledge that within us. If we are honest, we use our periods of waiting not to do self-examination, but often to draw others unto us, make them feel bad for us, and unite our own misery to theirs. Instead of giving us an emotional kick in the pants, they often also commiserate about their own waiting, their own discontents, and there we sit...in our misery.

No matter how much we gripe, complain, commiserate, or sit with others in shared misery, waiting doesn't hurry itself up. We still must wait, no matter how much we talk about it, dwell on it, think about it, or complain about it. It's probably safe to say we spend far more energy trying to avoid waiting or being upset about it than we do focused on the process and trusting God in and through it.

Instead of complaining, sharing, and making sure everyone knows just how unhappy we are in the waiting process, maybe it would be better to step back and look over our waiting period, seeing it for exactly what it is. It's a true fact to say we will probably spend a good portion of our lives waiting for one thing or another, so it would benefit us to learn how to handle our waiting periods. It's also true to say that waiting periods end, so for all we fuss about them, they aren't permanent states of being. No matter how long we stand in a waiting season, we know it can conclude. Thus, like all situations and seasons, it is to our benefit to seek out the best possible principles, spiritual education, and insights to see what this season is about. We will never do that if we complain about it so long, such overshadows the truth we need to see for our right here, and right now.

- 6 -
THERE ARE NO SECRETS

*Our inner selves wait [earnestly] for the Lord;
He is our Help and our Shield.
For in Him does our heart rejoice,
because we have trusted (relied on and been confident)
in His Holy name.
Let Your mercy and loving-kindness, O Lord, be upon us,
in proportion to our waiting and hoping for You.
(Psalm 33:20-22)*

- <u>Reading</u>: Galatians 6:7-12
- <u>Insight</u>: In waiting, wait it out.

People are always intrigued when self-help books come out that promise the "secrets" or "hidden truths" about situations. We love the idea that we can figure out the hidden mysteries of life and avoid difficulty, pain, or problems in the meantime. The concepts these writings expound are typically repetitive and so non-specific, they can relate to just about anything in one's life. People swear the "secrets" work, they do special practices that relate to them, and they go out and spend lots of money on the merchandise: T-shirts, bumper stickers, CDs, books, keychains, and anything that will remind them of ways to apply these specific secret truths in their lives.

As quickly as these ideas flow in trend, they often fall out of trend, very quickly. The reason why is no hidden mystery or secret: it's because they are nice ideas that often don't work. People will roll along, applying these different ideas to their lives, right until the day where they have a problem, a situation, or a circumstance to which the vague, leading ideas don't apply. I don't even think walking away from the trend is a conscious thing; it's just something that happens when someone realizes the ideas aren't working for them anymore. They might drift to another trend, or more than likely, wait for a while, adopt the concepts they always have, and then move on to something else. Their hopes and dreams of imagining wealth, having love, or success, without having to do anything, vanish as quickly as they came.

When it comes to waiting, there are no secrets. There are lots of books and opinions about "how we wait" or "what to do while waiting," but waiting appears to be the one thing that a lot of self-help advice just can't avoid. It's something all of us must do, and that means nobody gets out of life without waiting for something. We can't wish it away, hope it away, imagine it away, or visualize ourselves out of it. Waiting is waiting is waiting, and there are no clever, quick ways to make waiting cease, stop, or end, just because we dislike the experience we have while we wait.

The best advice I can give to anyone who must wait through a situation is simple: wait it out. It's not a secret; it's a reality. No one wants to put that slogan on merchandise, because it's not something that makes us feel good. Recognizing there are no secrets, we take a deep breath, and we wait. We focus on our purpose, we are consistent with our movements, and we trust that even though there's no secrets, waiting reflects life's truth.

– 7 –
ALL WE NEED IS JUST A LITTLE PATIENCE

> NEVER LAG IN ZEAL *AND* IN EARNEST ENDEAVOR;
> BE AGLOW *AND* BURNING WITH THE SPIRIT, SERVING THE LORD.
> REJOICE *AND* EXULT IN HOPE; BE STEADFAST AND PATIENT
> IN SUFFERING *AND* TRIBULATION; BE CONSTANT IN PRAYER.
> (ROMANS 12:11-12)

- <u>Reading</u>: Psalm 37:1-11
- <u>Insight</u>: Impatience doesn't make your wait any shorter.

I've heard talk over the years about people who are "naturally patient." In all these years of life and ministry, I have yet to meet anyone who I would describe as "naturally patient." No matter how laid back someone might appear to be, there is always some part of someone dying to get out, because they just can't stand back on the sidelines any longer. Most people, I'd venture to say, are rather impatient. They dislike processes, they dislike structure and order, and they strongly dislike anything that doesn't come to them immediately. In summary we could say this is all for one reason: people don't like to wait.

Human nature is inherently self-centered. Our immediate goal is ourselves; we want what we want when we want it. We dislike things such as structure and order because with them come policy and procedures, and those things force us to step back and wait things out while we grow into the needed maturity to carry whatever our ultimate goal might be. As we advance in different stages, we learn essential things about the world outside of us as well as ourselves that we can't learn if we rush ahead and have whatever we want immediately. Still, most humans jump at each and every chance to skip steps, have what they want now (even if it's not good for them) and avoid those important truths that keep them from both spiritual and self-discoveries.

Waiting brings out the inner impatience most, if not all, human beings carry. We are forced to wait for that reason: behind inner impatience are characteristics, flaws, and issues that need change, healing, and transformation. While we wait, our impatience comes out because we don't want to deal with the things about us that are just not ready to have whatever it is we seek. We don't want to go deep, for fear we will discover just how imperfect we are. Impatience hopes — and aspires — that we can skip such discomforts to get to just where we want to be, without those steps.

Problem is, we can't. Those parts of us that need to change still need to change, even if, in our impatience and haste, we can avoid going to the depths we hope to avoid. Patience is an important spiritual principle for this reason: it is trusting God enough to slow ourselves down, move at an eternal pace (rather than a timeline pace) rather than a chronological one, and be consistent in the call and purposes of God, no matter how long it takes. Through our wait, it benefits us to be patient and trusting, and learn just a little bit more how important process is to our spiritual journey.

– 8 –
I WON'T BACK DOWN

Do not, therefore, fling away your fearless confidence, for it carries a great and glorious compensation of reward. For you have need of steadfast patience and endurance, so that you may perform and fully accomplish the will of God, and thus receive and carry away [and enjoy to the full] what is promised.
(Hebrews 10:35-36)

- <u>Reading</u>: 2 Chronicles 15:1-14
- <u>Insight</u>: Don't back down unless God calls you to do so.

In my many years of ministry, perhaps the greatest challenge I see others face is the dedication of commitment. Whenever a period arises with little to no activity, especially when it coincides with a reasonably long wait, the commitment to the work often falters. It moves in stages: first the challenge is to get things moving, then it is to try and inspire new activity, then it follows with a long self-examination to try and fix things from within, and finally, a loss of interest, however temporary the waiting period may be. I've seen ministries more than falter in this process; I have seen them reduced to nothing, fail to continue, or sometimes, fall apart all together, all because the waiting process causes a minister to be discouraged to the point where they back down.

I am the first to admit that some situations come along to make us examine them, in depth. We aren't meant to take on every project or idea we pursue, and some things require us to walk away or leave them in favor of new projects or ideas that will bear better fruit. Overall, however, I find this to be an exception, rather than a rule. Much of the time, the things we desire to walk away from, let go of, be free of, or ignore require more of us than we anticipated. We are hoping that, if we can just let go of this ministry, this part of our lives, this relationship, this situation, or this circumstance, our "wait" will be over and we will no longer have to stand patient, deal with ourselves, or get real with God, like He desires.

Inclined to impatience, it's easy to think backing down from a circumstance or situation will keep us from having to wait longer, or more, or sometimes, ever again. Life, of course isn't that simple. If we stop waiting on one thing, something else will come along, forcing us to wait for that. Waiting doesn't end just because we give something up or look to something new. It is a process we must submit ourselves to, discipline ourselves through, and come out on the other side, learning and growing through our wait.

Don't allow a wait to make you think your whole life is on a wrong path. Hold fast and wait. This speaks volumes to commitment, consistency, and ability, even if you are having a difficult time. Through your wait, you may discover some things that need change. If you do, great; move to change them. Don't think the answer is to throw your whole life out and to start a new one. Realities speak: doing so will force you to wait all over again for something else on the other side. There is a sense of empowerment that comes when we stand fast during a wait, and it is only found therein.

− 9 −

UNLESS A GRAIN OF WHEAT FALLS

I ASSURE YOU, MOST SOLEMNLY I TELL YOU, UNLESS A GRAIN OF WHEAT FALLS INTO THE EARTH AND DIES, IT REMAINS [JUST ONE GRAIN; IT NEVER BECOMES MORE BUT LIVES] BY ITSELF ALONE. BUT IF IT DIES, IT PRODUCES MANY OTHERS AND YIELDS A RICH HARVEST.
(JOHN 12:24)

- <u>Reading</u>: 2 Corinthians 9:6-15
- <u>Insight</u>: Harvest always follows the "wait" after seedtime.

If you've spent any time in church over the past 30 or so years, you've probably heard a lot of talk about "sowing and reaping." The theory is that you reap what you sow, and that sowing and reaping are a spiritual process. Whatever you give to your spiritual process (sow) is what will come back to you (reap). There is truth in the teaching. It is Biblical to say that we will reap what we sow. The only problem with the teaching is that it is highly incomplete. If you listen to it long enough, it sounds like all you must do is put something out there and it will come back immediately. There is no instruction or consideration about actual agricultural process, for one simple reason: In agriculture, it's not as simple as sowing and reaping. There is a whole process in between, that involves the "w" word we all love: waiting.

The process for growing is as follows: sowing, dying, growing, living, and then reaping. In between sowing and reaping are three additional steps frequently skipped by preachers, because they know the middle part of the message won't be very popular. For a plant to grow, flourish, prosper, and thrive, a seed must first die, then sprout, and then live. We can't reap a seed; we must reap a plant. For us to reach harvest's point, we must follow the same process, and become something with the power to live.

We don't live without waiting. A seed has the potential and power to live, but that potential goes nowhere without the dedicated process of plant care. That seed must be planted in suitable soil that has been tilled and prepared to receive that seed. The seed must be then watered, even after it sprouts into a plant. The young sprouts need careful tending: you don't want to flood them with too much water, or not enough water. There is time and care to make sure conditions are just right to keep them growing: the right amount of sun, avoidance of pestilence or blight, and the perfect amount of water.

It takes a great amount of work to bring a plant to harvest. The work of fussing, tending, and care are all part of the long wait that moves between "sowing" and "reaping." It doesn't happen overnight. We don't just get instant results; we must wait. Just like with any plant, the wait is longer or shorter, depending on what that seed contains. Some seasons are short; some take much longer. Some engage more needed care, and some are easy and quick. Regardless, the promise is the same: the seed is sown, it dies, it grows, it lives, and then the plant is harvested. To get from sowing to reaping, we must wait.

– 10 –
UNSPOKEN CONVERSATIONS

[LIVING AS BECOMES YOU] WITH COMPLETE LOWLINESS OF MIND (HUMILITY) AND MEEKNESS (UNSELFISHNESS, GENTLENESS, MILDNESS), WITH PATIENCE, BEARING WITH ONE ANOTHER AND MAKING ALLOWANCES BECAUSE YOU LOVE ONE ANOTHER. BE EAGER AND STRIVE EARNESTLY TO GUARD AND KEEP THE HARMONY AND ONENESS OF [AND PRODUCED BY] THE SPIRIT IN THE BINDING POWER OF PEACE.
(EPHESIANS 4:2-3)

- <u>Reading</u>: Galatians 6:1-6
- <u>Insight</u>: Pay attention to "unspoken conversations" to find needed rest.

In the immediate days following my late husband's death, I didn't know what to say to other people. Their questions were invasive and uncomfortable. All I wanted – what I was waiting for – was to feel better and resume life as the person I used to be before he died. When this didn't happen (there was no way it would), I realized my waiting was in vain and waited, instead, to reach the point where I would feel like a new, or revived, person. The process wasn't quite like this, either. I often spent my days waiting, avoiding discussion with most people. I knew that most of the people I knew didn't understand, and talking to them would only make me feel worse.

What did help was the grace of what I now call "unspoken conversations." I met a widowed woman who had known my husband way back in their school days. When she told me that she, too had been widowed, I said to her, "Then you know what this is like." Her response to me was, "Every day." In this short exchange, barely two sentences long, we both said – and knew – everything we needed to know. She knew how I felt, she knew I was not able to explain it and didn't want to, and I knew that she knew what this was like, how hopeless it felt, and what it was like to wait, in vain, for a sense of change that would never come. We had the longest conversation imaginable in two sentences, all of it unspoken.

    I believe that beyond discomfort, much of our waiting experiences bring up things within us that we aren't easily able to explain to other people. They are things so deeply felt, so hard for us to process or address, we sometimes talk too much as we try to expound them for others. We hope that as we talk about them, way more than we should, others will feel a certain way toward us to alleviate our difficulties and pains. When this doesn't happen, we retreat to a place where we don't want to talk about it much, if at all, because the feeling of being misunderstood outweighs any hurt or discomfort we might encounter as we wait. Thus, we retreat.

    We know when people "get" our suffering and difficulties, even if they don't say very much. That's what makes unspoken conversations so special as we wait. They aren't wordy. They don't require any explanation. They are sacred, quiet, safe places where we know what we know what we know, and if someone doesn't know, they don't know. In our waiting, the unspoken becomes a place of safety and rest, where we can unburden ourselves and lay down the things that hurt us most, prepared to pick up better things for the future.

− 11 −
ONE MORE NIGHT

Show me Your ways, O Lord; teach me Your paths. Guide me in Your truth and faithfulness and teach me, for You are the God of my salvation; for You [You only and altogether] do I wait [expectantly] all the day long.
(Psalm 25:4-5)

- <u>Reading</u>: Matthew 6:25-34
- <u>Insight</u>: Living in the moment is more beneficial than living in the future.

Twelve-step programs are infamously known for their practice of taking things "one day at a time." The reason for this is simple: If an addict must face the idea of never having another drink again or never taking another drug for the rest of their lives, they will surely relapse. Instead, addicts are encouraged to learn how to take things one day at a time; one situation at a time; one circumstance at a time; and one experience at a time. Rather than fast-forward into the future, addicts learn how to be present right now. As they do so, they learn how to handle things one at a time. In a strange sense, they also learn how to wait.

One of the reasons we have a hard time with waiting is because we desire to be in a different point in our lives than we are. We think the answer to our longings and desires rest just beyond the horizon. It'll be in that new job, the bigger house in the better neighborhood, the next relationship, the pay raise, the better car, the new start, or whatever else we associate with a better option for ourselves. We are impatient to get to that perceived "answer" and we hate the idea that it doesn't come along and find us when we are ready for it. Thus, waiting runs day into day and night into night. The longer we go without whatever we are waiting for, the darker our experience can become.

We all have something to learn from those in 12-step recovery: the principle of being present now, instead of thinking and hoping our answers will be resolved by outside circumstances somewhere in the "beyond." We can start to manage our lives, one day at a time. In the case of the darkness of waiting, we must focus on getting through this night, just one more time. If we look over the whole of our wait with the hopes that something else will come along and fix it, our wait will be agonizing. It is far better for us to examine our wait day by day, live it now, and focus on where we are instead of where we always want to be in an endless drive to a perfection we cannot achieve.

Your problems will not be magically solved "over there." Every aspect of human life has challenges and complications. Yes, you might find yourself greatly blessed when you find what you seek, but you will also find new problems, issues, and things which you must wait to receive. When we take things one day (or night) at a time, it is much easier to assess our progresses and advances and look at our victories rather than our issues, our joys rather than our concerns, and come to a place of hope rather than despair.

− 12 −
SUFFERING

WHOEVER DOES NOT PERSEVERE AND CARRY HIS OWN CROSS AND COME AFTER (FOLLOW) ME CANNOT BE MY DISCIPLE.
(LUKE 14:27)

- <u>Reading</u>: 1 Peter 2:19-25
- <u>Insight</u>: Suffering reminds us of Christ; Christ reminds us of life.

"Suffering" is one of those words that makes the average person cringe. It's totally understandable why; nobody wants to be uncomfortable. The idea of having to suffer is unappealing on multiple levels…because suffering costs us something. Whether it costs us friendships, relationships, pleasures, enjoyments, or aspects of our lives we are simply unwilling to surrender, suffering is just something we could all live without.

If Jesus suffered for us, why didn't all suffering disappear? I think this is a fair question from a theological perspective, but let's be honest: no one asks this from a theological musing. We ask it from a place of discomfort, questioning the reason why we go through what we go through. There are often no, if any, satisfactory answers. Theologically, we know the entire world awaits final restoration. While Jesus has made the way for us to reach the Father, all our problems have not yet vanished while we live this side of heaven. Knowing this, however, doesn't make the experiences we suffer through feel any different. When we experience the powerful and painful sides of life, we do not seek theology; we seek remedy.

Waiting is a form of suffering for many, especially if we wait for an alleviation of some suffering. We find ourselves questioning, curious, interested, and preoccupied, all at the same time. Our focus can easily be on ourselves and what we are going through, to the exclusion of others and their own situations. It's easy to forget that everyone goes through something, and the confines of discomfort can make us think our suffering will never end.

When we suffer through something (yes, even an agonizing wait), it reminds us of the experience that Christ had while on this earth. We don't often consider it, but we do know that Christ was very aware the end of His earthly life would involve pain and suffering. As He taught, ate, instructed, spoke, prayed, and went about His regular life and ministry, He always knew what would await Him at the cross. Even though I don't believe Jesus was obsessed or fixated on it, He was, in a sense, waiting to complete the final action of redemption on our behalf. I'm sure there were times when Christ might have wanted to get matters over with, because He knew what He was to do would bring forth great glory. At the same time, Jesus had to wait — and maintain things in preparation for what was to come. Suffering is hard, no doubt, but sometimes it brings about a greater purpose. What greater purpose does your wait, your period of suffering, bring into this world?

– 13 –
LEARNING TO BE UNCOMFORTABLE

[YOU SHOULD] BE EXCEEDINGLY GLAD ON THIS ACCOUNT, THOUGH NOW FOR A LITTLE WHILE YOU MAY BE DISTRESSED BY TRIALS AND SUFFER TEMPTATIONS, SO THAT [THE GENUINENESS] OF YOUR FAITH MAY BE TESTED, [YOUR FAITH] WHICH IS INFINITELY MORE PRECIOUS THAN THE PERISHABLE GOLD WHICH IS TESTED AND PURIFIED BY FIRE. [THIS PROVING OF YOUR FAITH IS INTENDED] TO REDOUND TO [YOUR] PRAISE AND GLORY AND HONOR WHEN JESUS CHRIST (THE MESSIAH, THE ANOINTED ONE) IS REVEALED.
(1 PETER 1:6-7)

- <u>Reading</u>: Matthew 5:1-12
- <u>Insight</u>: Allow life to encourage you through the discomforts of waiting.

If you've ever had a rash, you know just how uncomfortable it can be. One of the most difficult things about rashes, regardless of their cause – allergies, illness, rosacea, dermatitis, eczema, psoriasis, bug bites, or things much like these – is that you aren't supposed to scratch them. It's understood that scratching can cause the skin to tear, and with the skin tearing causes greater potential for further irritation or infection. We spend millions of dollars annually trying to cure itch, however it comes, because we know that its annoyance leaves us in extreme discomfort.

If you study the backgrounds of many things that cause rashes, however, it's often safe to say that medicine doesn't have an answer for them. While medical advice might understand the basics of the irritation and what is happening, they often don't know why such things occur. Not every rash or itch is curable with calamine lotion or hydrocortisone cream. Even those that are curable through such means often have long-term foundations behind them that have no clear cause. In such instances, medicine offers treatments, but no cures.

When people deal with chronic itch, they learn to be uncomfortable. They find ways to subside it as much as possible, but they live with the long-term discomforts of something that doesn't have a simple answer. Most become very creative: they learn holistic methods to reduce inflammation, handle their diets differently or learn great make-up techniques to cover up redness. They meditate or talk to themselves through chronic itch. They learn the fine art of discomfort, because if they don't, they will find their entire lives revolve around their persistent conditions.

When we wait, we all learn a little bit more about the fine art of learning to be uncomfortable. Much like people with chronic conditions, we seek out answers in the beginning. Finding those answers might take the entirety of our lives for a little while, as we hope and wait for something that will make sense to us and end the circumstance to which we find ourselves. Then, as time goes on, we find that life has a way of taking itself back. We start having to live: pay bills, go to work, engage with other people, have conversations, and experience whatever life has to offer, while we wait. Sure, we are uncomfortable. Just like that persistent itching, we find ways to handle our discomfort. We pray more, we trust more, we read Scripture more frequently. The more we do, the better we feel, and the less our lives feel consumed by the discomfort of waiting.

- 14 -
ALL EYES ON YOU

> But I obtained mercy for the reason that in me,
> as the foremost [of sinners], Jesus Christ might show forth
> and display all His perfect long-suffering and patience
> for an example to [encourage] those who would thereafter
> believe on Him for [the gaining of] eternal life.
> (1 Timothy 1:16)

- <u>Reading</u>: Hebrews 6:1-15
- <u>Insight</u>: Wait well for yourself, not for everyone who might be watching.

When we discovered my late husband was dying of stage IV liver cancer, I found myself overwhelmed with the realities I now dreaded, because I knew they would come to pass. I knew I would be the one who would be with him in his final hours, ultimately when he died. I knew I'd have to confront his family after he died. I knew I'd have to face his memorial service; not just attending but presiding over it. At that point, I had no idea of how long it would be; where we would be financially or if things would arise that I wouldn't be able to handle. I was waiting for the inevitable, with a sense of dread and anxiety that couldn't be easily verbalized.

I didn't tell many people what was going on, for this very reason. I didn't know how to explain my concerns, my fears, my conflicting feelings to someone else. I told my best friend first. As we talked about things, she told me something very powerful: there would be many people watching me to see how I handled this situation. I knew when she told me that she was right. As I waited in this situation, one that was most complicated and painful, there were many people observing to see if what they believed about me was true, if I could measure up to the things they had heard about me, and if I lived both what I preach and claim to believe.

In a situation that was understandably difficult, where the realization of waiting made me feel conflicted and sometimes guilty, it wasn't easy to realize that all eyes were on me. Those moments, those days when I wanted to fall apart, I knew people were watching to see how I lived under the pressure. Whether I succeeded or failed, I can't say. I know what I lived as I waited, and I can say that I did the best I knew how to do. I waited; I handled each day that came; and through a lot of prayer and great conversations with the few I knew who understood, I waited while everyone watched.

I do know that when we are waiting, my experience wasn't that uncommon. People love to see how we do, what we do, if we can withstand the difficulties we find in waiting, and if we ultimately crack as we experience the trials we find as we wait. This is why it is so important to examine our wait, examine ourselves, and learn what we need to learn as we go through the experience. Waiting can be a powerful time of spiritual growth and insight, all had while we wait. Rather than proving ourselves to everyone else, if we wait well, we might just reveal something new about ourselves: how strong we can be.

- 15 -
EXPOSED!

NOTHING IS [SO CLOSELY] COVERED UP THAT IT WILL NOT BE REVEALED, OR HIDDEN THAT IT WILL NOT BE KNOWN. WHATEVER YOU HAVE SPOKEN IN THE DARKNESS SHALL BE HEARD AND LISTENED TO IN THE LIGHT, AND WHAT YOU HAVE WHISPERED IN [PEOPLE'S] EARS AND BEHIND CLOSED DOORS WILL BE PROCLAIMED UPON THE HOUSETOPS.
(LUKE 12:2-3)

- Reading: Isaiah 20:1-16
- Insight: Embrace exposure to see just what you need to change.

There's an aspect of waiting, seldom discussed, but very real, nonetheless. It brings us to our knees, right to the place of realization waiting is designed to direct. We come to know our limitations. We know what must change, even if we don't know in the here and now just how to do it. In waiting, our awareness is heightened. Suddenly, we are exposed.

All is put out there for us to see. We are forced to deal with aspects of our lives that we would rather not, and we are face-to-face with the darker parts of ourselves, the parts of us that don't get redeemed as quickly as others. We are forced into a place of self-examination, because we are now seeing clearly. It's not all about everyone else, it's not about everyone who doesn't give us our way...it's now about us.

Exposure isn't an experience most long to have. It's something, if we are to be quite honest, most go out of their way to avoid. We don't like the feeling of having our issues, matters, and situations laid bare, to be seen. It makes us feel like we've been found out, revealed, unveiled, can't run, and can't hide. Because we are waiting, we can't hide behind the future or the past. We must stand, experience, and encounter the exposure that is for our own good...even if it doesn't feel like it.

The Scriptures tell us the Prophet Isaiah walked around naked for three years. Beyond the obvious question: Why would God ask someone to do this, rests the reality of exactly what the Prophet Isaiah did with his very literal actions. By walking around naked, the prophet showed Isaiah the principle of literal exposure. Before God, the Israelites were bare: the good, bad, and indifferent. Their sins were visible, real, and aware. As perfect as they might have seemed to everyone else, they needed God's help and His intervention to overcome the things that kept them from Him. They were exposed, there was no way they could hide it, and they had to confront it.

There is no greater example of our needed changes, issues, wants, and improvements than those which surface when we are forced to wait. They are exposed for our insight, to give us something to attend to, deal with, experience, and handle as we wait for something else, better, transformative, or different. The change we experience as we wait doesn't come just from the newness of the season that lies ahead; it also comes, just as much, from the process we are willing to undertake as we wait. Exposure never feels good, but it is real, and definitely honorable. We can't change what we hide, and we can't hide what is exposed.

− 16 −
IT IS WHAT IT IS

*IT IS GOOD FOR ME THAT I HAVE BEEN AFFLICTED,
THAT I MIGHT LEARN YOUR STATUTES.
(PSALM 119:71)*

- <u>Reading</u>: John 16:18-33
- <u>Insight</u>: Believe the facts about yourself.

When my late husband first died, I assumed my life would, at some point in time, resume the course it had prior to his death. This, of course, was totally unrealistic. I waited with the hope that one day, I would feel the way I used to about life, myself, and things in general. I figured this new way of looking at the world, of feeling about my life and relationships in general, and the assessments I had about my marriage would quickly fade, dissolve, and change after some magical moment when all would seem better, normal, and familiar, once again.

It was unrealistic for me to think my life and outlook on life would be what it once was. I waited, unsuccessfully, for things to be other than what they now were. I was an example of someone who underwent a powerful change, entered a new phase of my life, and wanted the old part of it back. I didn't like how I felt, I didn't like the way things were, and I didn't like the new pressures I suddenly felt. I also didn't like, as I struggled to reconcile my husband's death with our very long and difficult marriage, the conflicts that would result. I was so deeply grieved by his death and the trauma that surrounded it, but I also couldn't deny the realities I lived with during our relationship. In some ways, I missed him. In some ways, I also could see I was more of myself without his presence in my life. This tore me up inside, wracked me with guilt, and left me feeling even more like I wanted my life, my perspective, and my situation to be what it once was.

Over and over again I've received the same advice, just in different words. What I lived with, what I recognize now, and what I feel now is what it is. My challenge is to let things be what they are, without attaching a lot of personal sentiment to them. Some things are facts, plain and simple. While we wait, we learn to let things be what they are, as those facts fall into place. Once we do this, we can see an important part of our journey that can never be overstepped, slighted, or skipped.

As people, we must learn to accept the facts that are our lives. Not every aspect of our lives exists in a parallel universe of emotions and feelings. Some things are just facts, part of what we speak of as "living life on life's terms." Waiting tends to cause us to overthink the facts of our lives, attaching all sorts of ideas and concepts to them that don't help our process, nor our acceptance. Yet while we wait, we should aspire to gain a better sense of those facts. When we can see things as they are, rather than as we are, it makes a huge difference in what we can withstand and see for ourselves for whatever comes next.

– 17 –
THE TREASURES OF DARKNESS

> AND I WILL GIVE YOU THE TREASURES OF DARKNESS
> AND HIDDEN RICHES OF SECRET PLACES, THAT YOU MAY KNOW
> THAT IT IS I, THE LORD, THE GOD OF ISRAEL, WHO CALLS YOU
> BY YOUR NAME.
> (ISAIAH 45:3)

- <u>Reading</u>: John 1:1-13
- <u>Insight</u>: The dark night of the soul does not last forever.

My spiritual daughter and I often talk about the world of "dark emotions." We discuss them, in favor of other things, for one simple reason: dark emotions are part of life, and they have a way of being ignored, shunned, pushed aside, and avoided by most people. We dislike such feelings because they bring us to places of truth and realization, but in a hard way, through a hard place. We've both taken note that the world of darkness is quickly avoided, and people will do just about anything to keep from feeling those difficult hardships. Having to wait through them, for most people, is considered agonizing.

When people talk about "the dark night of the soul," they are talking about a waiting period in life that is plagued by dark emotions. It's often a period that brings a person into deep thoughts, especially about the meaning of life and their best placement therein. Things feel murky, rather than clear. There doesn't seem to be an obvious way out of the situation. They see themselves in a difficult and unyielding light, and the truth they uncover is dark and brooding. While they process, they wait, uncomfortable, unyielding, in a dark and difficult place.

There is something we gain from dealing with darkness, however. We find the "treasures of darkness;" the beauty that exists in waiting periods full of sadness, grief, despair, and longing for light. There is something profound that happens as we wrestle and come out on the other side, because we can't find the light of God if we don't first see and experience the darkness. The Scriptures tell us that light shines in the darkness, which means we must first find darkness to embrace the light. We must hold true and embrace the truths we find revealed in the dark, quiet places of our reality to fully embrace what God does and brings to light.

Darkness never feels like a treasure when we wait through it. We rest in the realities that are just God and us, unable to blame anyone else, see anyone else, or point the finger elsewhere. He gets us in a place where we wrestle with ourselves, come out on the other side, and find the truth in the light. It's a process, one that takes as long as it takes, that can't be sped up. We must wait through it, acknowledging our Creator knows the beginning from the end. We shall see the light when the dawn breaks, embracing and holding the treasures we've come to acquire from the lengthy wait in darkness that provided the means to come and receive God's light to us in a new and profound way.

– 18 –
UNSATISFACTORY ANSWERS

You know how we call those blessed (happy) who were steadfast [who endured]. You have heard of the endurance of Job, and you have seen the Lord's [purpose and how He richly blessed him in the] end, inasmuch as the Lord is full of pity and compassion and tenderness and mercy.
(James 5:11)

- <u>Reading</u>: Job 38:1-41
- <u>Insight</u>: Accept God's answer to wait as sufficient.

"When will we be there?" "When we get there." "But why can't I do it?" "Because I said so." "But it's not fair!" "Life is not fair!"

From the time we were very young, we learned the reality that life, nor people, aren't always quick to provide us with satisfactory answers. When we are waiting, especially if we are waiting on something we think we want, we don't like the feeling of being held back. Our verbal protests indicate our thorough dissatisfaction with our circumstances. We want to know why we can't do something, why it is taking so long to come to pass, or why we are having to experience a situation that feels nothing more than unfair. Even as adults, we still find ourselves as pouting children, crossing our arms and stomping our feet in defiance, because we aren't getting whatever it is we want.

Waiting teaches us that some things don't have satisfactory answers. We see this nowhere better than in Job's experience, recorded in forty chapters of trauma, self-discovery, divine wisdom, and a whole lot of waiting. We like to focus on the fact that Job's wait ended with abundance, but we skip the part where Job waited...and waited...and waited. This unique piece of ancient Scripture shows us Job's process as well as his promise, and just how his wait changed him in a powerful and profound way.

Job's experience shows us it's not the answers that are wrong, but often our questions. We don't get the answers we hope to receive in a waiting period because we must learn to accept God is our Lord, in both seasons we enjoy and seasons we find distressing. Waiting teaches us acceptance, acceptance of circumstance and of the authority of God within our lives. When we were children and we received unsatisfactory answers from the adults in our lives, they established authority in our lives. We didn't need to have all the answers, nor did we have to receive answers that made us happy; we just had to receive an answer. Now, as those walking with God, we just have to receive an answer from God as sufficient to know that, satisfactory to us or not, we are within God's purpose now, in this time, to wait. We talk much about the Lordship of God, but we see it nowhere greater, and adopt it nowhere better, than when we accept God's answer that for right now, like it or not, we must stand fast and wait.

– 19 –

GREAT EXPECTATIONS

He who is slow to anger is better than the mighty,
he who rules his [own] spirit than he who takes a city.
(Proverbs 16:32)

- <u>Reading</u>: Romans 12:9-17
- <u>Insight</u>: Wait through your unmet expectations to find real truth.

I read somewhere that the number one killer of relationships is unmet expectations. The reason these expectations are usually unmet is because no one ever voices them. They are there, brewing under the surface, but never spoken. After a stretch of unsuccessful waiting, the relationship blows up, much like the unmet expectations. In that waiting comes frustration and angst, often that could be resolved with a conversation rather than a brewing, stewing opposition to an unreasonable circumstance.

If we are honest, we, as people, carry many great and lofty expectations throughout our lives. Our expectations are an overflow of our personal esteem of ourselves: they reflect what we think we deserve or need, and what we expect someone else to pour out, model back, or reflect of ourselves to us. Sometimes our expectations are justified; sometimes they are not high enough; but other times, our expectations are unreasonably high. They spill over, pouring out on our co-workers, friends, family, and family in Christ. When they don't get met, we get upset...and unsuccessfully wait for them to come to fruition.

It is in those times of waiting that our expectations are addressed, often in ways we dislike. We don't want to deal with that we might think too highly of ourselves or that maybe our expectations in general are unreasonable in some way. We don't want to sit and face that maybe we expect God to do things that He is neither obligated to do, nor going to do, for us. We love the ideas of being established and worthy and fantastic, but we hate the place of humbling, of learning to find that balance between improper esteem and inflated self-value.

When we wait, we are automatically humbled. The great, exalted things we think of ourselves must take their place: they too, must wait. It doesn't matter if we have the highest earthly position or the lowest one imaginable: we still must wait. Our expectations find a place of grounding, allowing them to be more reasonable. This enhances our relationship with God, as well as our relationship with others.

When we set aside our "great expectations," we are better able to find ourselves, for ourselves. We are face-to-face with God in the way He desires: honest, raw, real, and truthful. Behind our expectations we find our failings, fears, flaws and emptiness, longing to be filled by all the wrong things. While we wait, we get real about who we are and what we are made of, and lay aside everything that hinders, hides, and conceals the truth about us to ourselves and others. Being made bare, we can now expect whatever is realistic.

– 20 –

ALL THAT YOU CAN'T LEAVE BEHIND

So you also must be patient. Establish your hearts [strengthen and confirm them in the final certainty], for the coming of the Lord is very near.
(James 5:8)

- <u>Reading</u>: Ephesians 4:13-24
- <u>Insight</u>: See what you gain as you transform through your wait.

It's my personal belief that we dislike waiting because we fear what it will cost us. Not only do we confront the extremes of the unknown, but we also confront the unknown, believing we will come out on the other side with less than we now have. Waiting can come with a period marked by loss, even if we never lose anything in the material or physical realm. If we wait, and wait right, we come to a place of profound change. Not everyone is on board when we change. We may lose friends, family members, and sometimes we even lose a sense of ourselves.

When we talk about waiting, we are quick to expound upon specific characteristics and virtues we associate with waiting. Waiting doesn't just call for patience; it often calls for a sense of death to everything that keeps us from moving into whatever might be next for us. Our focus is often on what we are losing. We stand and look out and can't believe we have lost so much. As a result, we don't feel like ourselves anymore. We just feel void, lost, uncomfortable, and uncertain about what is to come.

The goal of waiting is to bring us to a place where we can handle what is next, while becoming more authentically who we are supposed to be at the same time. At the end of our wait might be difficulty, rather than the sense of concluded victory we hope to achieve. We don't know what lies ahead, at least in the immediate sense, while we wait.

What we gain through a wait, however, is what we use to handle whatever is next. It doesn't matter what it is; we know we can handle it, we can experience it, and we are fully equipped for it. We can't leave behind the character, growth, and insights we've received, because they are there, specifically for the purpose of whatever lies ahead. It isn't the most comfortable experience imaginable to develop the things we must, because they come through profound examination and realization. We need to realize we won't be totally void of who we are when we make it to the other side. We will be shaped, transformed, and created into something new, while still being ourselves. We will just have the opportunity to be more of who we are, because we have come to know and embrace it better than we have in the past.

There is no denial we change in waiting, and that in changing, we do lose certain things. There is so much to be said, though, for all we gain. We must put some things down, away, and aside to grow into all we become. Then we get to the part where we hold, even more, to all the things we can't leave behind.

– 21 –

THE FULLNESS OF TIME

*BY YOUR STEADFASTNESS AND PATIENT ENDURANCE
YOU SHALL WIN THE TRUE LIFE OF YOUR SOULS.
(LUKE 21:19)*

- <u>Reading</u>: Galatians 4:1-8
- <u>Insight</u>: The fullness of time is an experience in eternity, rather than chronology.

All of us have started projects, jobs, or ideas that just don't seem to take off when we start them. We might find ourselves frustrated and aggravated, hoping that if we keep pushing, the product will turn into whatever we'd originally envisioned. When this doesn't happen, we can easily feel dismayed and as if we should do nothing more than give everything up and take on something else.

In my many years of ministry, this is the typical response I see to difficulties that arise in ministry. Instead of sitting back, waiting, praying, and seeking God, the answer is to drop a project, start a whole new vision or idea, or begin something else. Over and over again, I see new projects, new ministry names, new identities, and new things…accompanied with a long trail of unfinished things that follow behind more things that never come to fruition.

When things come along that just don't work out, what should we do? Should we start over again, doing something entirely different? Should we push harder?

what we should do in such times is wait. In waiting, we can begin our long-fought process to hear from God about whatever it may be that we've undertaken. It may not be that the project or idea itself is a problem, but maybe it's just not the right time to do it. It could also be that maybe the basic project or idea is there, but maybe you're not going about it quite right at this time. It's very possible that your project, or situation, or circumstance has not found its "fullness of time" yet, and that means...you need to wait.

The Scriptures tell us Jesus came when the "fullness of time was come." This tells us that God does things at the perfect time (yes, even the coming of Christ); when they are ready to be embraced, received, and understood. Not every time is the perfect time to do something, undertake something, or start something. Often we press and push to do things that are not the right time to do, simply because we don't want to wait.

Divine timing is about more than just us being ready for something. It also considers the situation within the world, spiritual and external factors that are now, and are to come, and receptivity of those who shall hear and receive. Just as the world needed to be ready to receive Christ, so too everyone and everything around us must be ready to receive our project, purpose, or mission. In the meantime, we wait. We wait well. We wait with anticipation. We wait with hope. We wrestle the darkness and come out prepared for life lived ready, now in the fullness of time.

– 22 –

HOLY GROUND

> WHEN MOSES SAW IT, HE WAS ASTONISHED *AND* MARVELED
> AT THE SIGHT; BUT WHEN HE WENT CLOSE TO INVESTIGATE,
> THERE CAME TO HIM THE VOICE OF THE LORD, SAYING,
> I AM THE GOD OF YOUR FOREFATHERS, THE GOD OF ABRAHAM AND OF
> ISAAC AND OF JACOB. AND MOSES TREMBLED *AND* WAS SO TERRIFIED
> THAT HE DID NOT VENTURE TO LOOK. THEN THE LORD SAID TO HIM,
> REMOVE THE SANDALS FROM YOUR FEET, FOR THE PLACE WHERE
> YOU ARE STANDING IS *HOLY GROUND AND* WORTHY OF VENERATION.
> (ACTS 7:31-33)

- <u>Reading</u>: Exodus 3:1-10
- <u>Insight</u>: Take your shoes off, for the place you now stand is holy.

When we think of the term "holy ground," we automatically think of Moses. Standing out in the desert, Moses found a burning bush, one that was lit on fire but didn't burn to ashes. The voice within the bush (clearly the voice of God) told him to remove his shoes, for the place he stood was holy ground. We love the idea of this; the concept of a humble shepherd out in a dry place, minding his own business and finding God there, in his midst. What we don't often consider are the circumstances surrounding Moses' encounter with God. The ground became holy because God was present, as Moses waited around, tending to the sheep, uncluttered in his mind, doing the last thing he was assigned to do before a new task came to him.

That ground in the desert wasn't holy because it

was the desert or because it was a plot of land marked exclusively for specialness. The ground in the desert was holy because God was present there, and God was acknowledged as being there. In that dry, difficult place, God made Himself known. Even though He could have manifested in the middle of a city or in a place where many people could have known and recognized that His presence alone creates holiness in a situation or circumstance, He didn't. Instead, God appeared to Moses in the loneliest, driest, and most patient place around. Why is this?

The desert is used in Biblical analogy to show us places of emptiness. We go to the desert to empty ourselves of everything that keeps us from God, because we find there are no distractions there. It is analogous to the same concept as darkness; we find ourselves there, undistracted, with no one else to blame, no one to keep us from God, and ultimately, I believe, to separate us. The true definition of "holiness" is "separateness." This doesn't mean we are separated to be better than anyone else or to ignore the rest of the world. No! It's that such a period of time is specific to discovering things about ourselves and find our true need for God in this distracting and often hurtful world. As we wait, we find ourselves in desert places; in those that help us to sit with God undistracted, focused, and knowing better who we are and what we are called to be than prior.

Wherever God is, we find holy ground. God is holy in our wait; and our space, our place, our time of waiting, is too, holy ground. This is our time of awe, to see God for ourselves, still burning and active in that bush, even today. He will come when no one else is around, just to show you that He is real and He is there, even when it feels like life has gone empty.

- 23 -

HOPE

BUT IF WE HOPE FOR WHAT IS STILL UNSEEN BY US, WE WAIT FOR IT WITH PATIENCE AND COMPOSURE.
(ROMANS 8:25)

- <u>Reading</u>: Ecclesiastes 2:17-25
- <u>Insight</u>: See moments of hope throughout your day.

"Hope" is probably not the first word you think of while waiting. Waiting can, in reality, cause us to feel the opposite of hope. I know that in many periods of waiting, I've felt a profound sense of hopelessness. This is not uncommon; when we wait, we don't know what we don't know. In order to have hope, we often assume we must know the end from the beginning, and see our way out of wherever we are.

It's true that knowing the outcome of a wait may indeed help with hope, but it could also lead to greater discouragement. What we wait for is not always what we receive. I believe in waiting, we are supposed to learn how to see hope in a different way; in a simple, everyday context rather than in the light of a huge event or something that causes a waiting period to end. It is God's will we learn to see Him everywhere, and in many different places and ways. When we do this, we are able to have hope, regardless of what might be going on around us.

Waiting forces us to slow down and live in the

moment. It is only when we live right now, in this moment and not the next, that we can enjoy the company of those who care enough to support us through this time. We suddenly notice the colors of the flowers, the warmth of the sun, the blessing of a great meal, the power of fellowship, and the general enjoyment life has to offer us, when we least expect it. In these little moments, we find encouragement and hope. Our wait doesn't seem so taxing, and as dark as our world may feel, we see a little bit of light peeking out over our seemingly impossible, never-ending night.

We don't need big events to feel hopeful. That might seem like the way to go, but it's not. We want big things, big moments; God expects us to learn about the little moments, those that take us from where we are to where we need to be, moment by moment. We gain far more encouragement, insight, and empowerment through what we go through if we are willing to receive these little moments of hopeful encouragement as we go along.

Life is never going to be perfect, even when your waiting period ends. Life will forever be full of need for spiritual insights, hopeful experiences, and little bits and pieces of divine light scattered through your days, there to help you remember God is with you, even as you sometimes stand, wait, and experience life in a dark, difficult place.

- 24 -

PARADIGM SHIFT

In those days there appeared John the Baptist, preaching in the wilderness (desert) of Judea and saying, Repent (think differently; change your mind, regretting your sins and changing your conduct), for the kingdom of heaven is at hand.
(Matthew 3:1-12)

- <u>Reading</u>: 2 Corinthians 4:11-18
- <u>Insight</u>: Avoid the distractions that often come through other people.

Whenever I picture John the Baptist, I imagine him completely wild and untamed. He ate funny things, he dressed funny and looked funny, and he moved with a power unseen in his day. He came out of the wilderness (seemingly out of nowhere) to preach a wild message: repentance. His message of repentance wasn't just random, however. He didn't just preach repentance for repentance's sake, but because there was something important coming behind it: the Kingdom of heaven was at hand. As close and as near as one could touch, the Kingdom of God was waiting and ready. The system, or paradigm, as they knew it, was shifting. A new day, a new way was coming.

We love this point of the story, because we know Christ was ready to step into the scene and transform all of us. What rested just before it, however, was a long wait while John hung out in the wilderness, becoming the image that was ready to change the world as he preached this powerful, new paradigm. Before he could preach about the shift, he had to first shift, himself.

It's not an accident that both John and Jesus spent time in the wilderness, sometimes translated as the desert, before beginning their active work in ministry. They went to the place with nothing to find everything and got themselves grounded for the difficulties that would lie ahead with the impending shift. They needed the ability to focus while they waited, and everything and everyone around them would be too tempting to stand as a distraction. Those around them needed their message as much as anyone else would, and they couldn't deal with influence and thought that might take them from the focus of their important task.

Sometimes we don't just wait for ourselves; we also wait for the quality of our purpose, our message or work. When we have something important to announce, such as a powerful shift, we can't miss step with God in any shape or form. We need our period of wait to rest, to hear from God, to sit in place, and to be still, no matter how dark or difficult our wait may prove to be. We must know when we've heard from God or when we have not, and we must wait through our difficult points and places to discipline ourselves to learn everything we should about our upcoming assignment. In waiting, we gain insight, wisdom, and teaching that can't come from a book. We come to discover the assignment itself, and how important the shifting paradigm is, that is to come.

- 25 -

VEILED IN SILENCE

When He [the Lamb] broke open the seventh seal, there was silence for about half an hour in heaven.
(Revelation 8:1)

- <u>Reading</u>: Job 34:29-37
- <u>Insight</u>: Be still and let God move.

The Isaacs' song, *Stand Still (and Let God Move)* speaks of the periods in life when we don't have clear direction about our next movements. When faced with such situations, we often wrestle in the silent discomfort that waiting delivers to us. I've found that people tend to dislike silence. This is because most of us grew up with the impression that silence equated to anger. We assume that silence in any form is a passive-aggressive message, loaded to the brim with everything someone wants to say, but isn't saying it. As a result, we are uncomfortable with silence. We don't like when things get too quiet, because we think that means something is wrong...someone is mad at us...maybe even God doesn't have anything nice to say about us, right now.

Our response is to fill our world with endless noise: noise at home, noise at work, noise in the car, noise online, even noise in church. We love the songs that are cranked up as loud as we can stand them so we won't have to hear the quiet silence that we associate with discomfort. We love our noise. We dislike our silence.

And yet, while we wait...that's what we find: silence.

we find the very thing that makes us the most uncomfortable, there to experience. We don't get insight or revelation until it is time for it to come. We must sit in the quiet, in the silence, in the place where we don't hear or recognize a clear direction. We must be still. We can't run ahead, because there is nothing to see in the distance. We are left, often feeling void, because while we wait, God very often comes to us in silence.

We have two choices when it comes to a silent wait: either fight it or align with it. If we fight it, we will miss the message when its time comes. We won't know God has come to show us, teach us, or reveal to us, because we will be too busy entertaining all our noise. If we align with it, we will find ourselves standing still, waiting for God to move. We will be ready to hear, to assemble, and to move forward.

Silence does not automatically mean or indicate God is angry. The silence in waiting is for the development of deep wisdom and insight, ideas and thoughts that cannot come about through great noise. The veil of silence protects us as we transform and grow in God. When we are ready to hear, God will speak. When we are ready to move forward, God will hasten our feet to move and live in Him, drawing on the powerful experience of silence.

– 26 –

THE SIGN OF JONAH

> THEN SOME OF THE SCRIBES AND PHARISEES SAID TO HIM, TEACHER, WE DESIRE TO SEE A SIGN OR MIRACLE FROM YOU [PROVING THAT YOU ARE WHAT YOU CLAIM TO BE]. BUT HE REPLIED TO THEM, AN EVIL AND ADULTEROUS GENERATION (A GENERATION MORALLY UNFAITHFUL TO GOD) SEEKS AND DEMANDS A SIGN; BUT NO SIGN SHALL BE GIVEN TO IT EXCEPT THE SIGN OF THE PROPHET JONAH.
> (MATTHEW 12:38-39)

- <u>Reading</u>: Jonah 2:1-10
- <u>Insight</u>: The sign of Jonah calls us. Will you answer to find God's truth?

The book of Jonah could be described as "the story of Jonah being headstrong and difficult." The Prophet Jonah was told by God to fulfill a specific assignment: go to the people of Nineveh and preach to them of impending destruction, which would come upon them due to their idolatrous and wicked ways. Jonah didn't want to do it. He took comfort in his own ideas that moving in the opposite direction of obedience (disobedience) would be all right with God, so he openly defied God's command to Him and went a different way.

Jonah's behavior didn't go without consequence, and he found himself in the middle of a storm, thrown overboard into the sea, and then sitting in the belly of a large fish for three days and nights, contemplating his life. It's easy enough to say Jonah was forced to wait in a dark, disgusting place for three days because he disobeyed God. Surely this is a conclusion we could reach, but God wanted to do something deeper in Jonah than just make sit in "time out" over disobedience. God wanted Jonah to examine his life, his beliefs and ideas, to see exactly how he got to such a difficult and intense place of gritty and honest waiting.

Every one of us has been Jonah. We don't like to think about that, but it's true. Every one of us has had an incident or a period in our lives where we just don't want to do what God asks of us, and we think we can just get by if we try hard enough. Sometimes, like it or not, God must bring us to a place of deep, dark waiting. Here, no matter how long it lasts, we can think about something other than our accomplishments. It doesn't matter how many spiritual successes we have or how many things we've done that get accolades and attention. All that matters is who we truly are, behind those things that cause others to take notice of us. We are called to a place of reality, and therein, we sit, and we wait.

We all know Jonah's three days and three nights in the belly of the fish represent the death of Christ; his rising up is a type of Christ's resurrection. The same is true for us. While we stay in a place of waiting, far away from everything that is familiar to us, we can think on just how much of our formation avoids the things of God because they easily distract us. Anyone can, within the span of a tradition, tell us something is God, when it's not. It is in these waiting places we learn what is God from what is not and embrace it for ourselves.

Every one of us needs the sign of Jonah: to make us wait, in the dark, for a personal resurrection experience. Every one of us needs to become one, so we can learn to distinguish what is God from what is not God in our lives.

– 27 –

NEW WINE

So for the sake of your tradition (the rules handed down by your forefathers), you have set aside the word of God [depriving it of force and authority and making it of no effect].
(Matthew 15:6)

- <u>Reading</u>: Matthew 9:14-17
- <u>Insight</u>: After transformation, you will find your spiritual flow.

It's not uncommon to hear church preaching or messages that expound on the principles of "new seasons" and "new starts." We don't often get to the actual teaching about such things, because people are so insanely excited about the idea of something new and different in their lives, their enthusiasm overshadows the structure and discipline of the message. We don't hear important teaching about waiting, producing, and coming to the place of "new wine" in our lives, because it's not the part of the message that gets a shout. It is the part of the message, though, that is so vitally essential. If we want to come to the point of newness, we must deal with the process to become new.

The Scriptures tell us that we should never put "new wine in old wineskins." We know it's telling us we can't put a new spiritual process into an old one. What we don't think about is the long waiting process involved from grape to wineskin, all of which change the very form of the grape. Grapes are harvested, juiced, pulverized, pressed, and crushed, all to make a liquid, a juice. The very form of the grapes change. While still their same essence, they have become something different, unrecognizable, and yes, new. Wine is nothing more than a bunch of grapes that have been transformed. They underwent a difficult process that changed them, allowing what was within them to flow.

Many of us want new things, but we don't want the process we must undergo to receive them. We don't want to wait through the pressing, crushing difficulties that leave us unlike the person we used to be. We want to flow, we want to be different, we want to be transformed, but we don't want the process to transform us. Problem is, we can't become wine if we refuse to remain as grapes. If we want a new thing, we must become the thing we desire to be. The only thing that shall transform us in this way...is time.

It is our traditions, our old ways of thinking, that keep us bound up as grapes long after it's time to turn into wine. We like to wrap ourselves in the way we were, the way things used to be, maybe even the hopes that if we hold on hard enough, they can be that way again. We cannot flow as we should if we are not pressed; we cannot change if we are not crushed; and we cannot flow if we refuse to wait out the difficult things that change us. Our form changes to release our true essence, that which lies within and God desires to bring forth. We will learn far more, move into greater places and do much more profound things if we transform...but only if we are willing to wait out our transformation.

– 28 –

THE WAITING IS THE HARDEST PART

[WHAT, WHAT WOULD HAVE BECOME OF ME] HAD I NOT BELIEVED THAT I WOULD SEE THE LORD'S GOODNESS IN THE LAND OF THE LIVING! WAIT AND HOPE FOR AND EXPECT THE LORD; BE BRAVE AND OF GOOD COURAGE AND LET YOUR HEART BE STOUT AND ENDURING. YES, WAIT FOR AND HOPE FOR AND EXPECT THE LORD.
(PSALM 27:13-14)

- <u>Reading</u>: Ecclesiastes 12:6-14
- <u>Insight</u>: Waiting is part of life, so learn to wait well.

The book of Ecclesiastes is seldom heard from the pulpit because its contents are heavy, weighty subject matter that must be studied to be understood. If there was one way I could summarize the book of Ecclesiastes, I'd say it is a call to pay attention to the "journey," rather than the destination. In this world, where we face time in a linear series of events rather than eternal understanding, we don't like journeys. We think of our circumstances to fall into "before" and "after," and we want to get from the first thing to the last thing, immediately. We don't consider the in-between part, the waiting part, to be of justifiable value. It's just before and after, with no aforethought of the middle.

We don't like the "middle" because it's the hard part. Waiting is hard because it's not our before and after. We can't mark our accomplishments by waiting periods; only by where we start and end. It's here, in this hard place, that we grow and change, we learn and develop, and we see God differently than we did prior. It's not a period marked by great fanfare, because no one sees what we are doing while we go through it. We go through much of our process alone. It's just us and God, changing and transforming to find the promise ahead that we can't yet see, but know, and believe, is there.

All throughout Scripture, we see great attention paid to "middle" times, to those hard periods of waiting. The Israelites had to wait for their ultimate liberation from Pharaoh. They spent 40 years wandering in the wilderness, waiting for their entry into the Promised Land. Job spent an extended period of time waiting on God to redeem him from a demonically imposed trial. The Israelites longed for freedom when they lived under captivity. The people of God waited 4,000 years to receive the promised Messiah. Now, we await Christ's return. We spend much of our lives, our time, our existence in these waiting places.

The waiting is the hardest part because it is life. We will forever await something, even if it's nothing more than the return of our Savior, and the ultimate redemption of our world. That's why books like Ecclesiastes and other passages with a similar message exist in Scripture. We have to learn how to wait, as we do this waiting thing right. Waiting is life; and in that life, we come to find God in a powerful way we otherwise would miss or avoid.

The victory isn't the next phase, the new season, or the end destination, as we are often told. It is the ability to wait through that hard part to come out on the other side as something different than when we started.

– AFTERWORD –

WHEN GOD GIVES THE DARKNESS

*AND THE LIGHT SHINES ON IN THE DARKNESS,
FOR THE DARKNESS HAS NEVER OVERPOWERED IT [PUT IT OUT
OR ABSORBED IT OR APPROPRIATED IT, AND IS UNRECEPTIVE TO IT].
(JOHN 1:5)*

Light doesn't shine in light. This is one of those facts we never think about, because we are accustomed to the science of electricity. Unless we are in a low light structure, we don't use the overhead lights or a lamp during the day. We don't use our car's headlights during daylight hours. No one needs a flashlight to navigate the street during morning or afternoon hours. We use light when it's dark to help us see, because light shines in darkness. To see the benefit of light, we must first see, and acknowledge, the darkness.

The Scriptures tell us that God created both light and dark, day and night. We've come to associate light with positivity and dark with negativity or evil, because we can't see where we are going or the results of situations when we are in darkness. As a result of our associations, we don't consider that darkness is needed as much as light, and darkness is part of our spiritual journey just as much as light. Darkness teaches us about faith, about hope, about life itself. God gives us darkness to help us find, see, and recognize the light.

The catch to darkness is that darkness doesn't understand the light. When we are in difficult or dark places, we don't understand what God is doing. We can't easily see our way to imagine anything good will come out of a long wait, because while we are in our situation, all we see and feel is the darkness. We can't see what God is doing, nor can we feel it. We find ourselves encompassed and engulfed by something that seems to take us far away from where we think we want to be.

We can't see the light if we never experience the darkness. Where we think we should be, what we think we should experience, and how we think we can get there are often quite different than the realities that emerge. In thinking that life will move from where we stand to where we hope to be in a straight line, we are caught off guard when we must make twists, turns, backflips, and long, extended marches in the dark. Nobody likes a dark, long experience that requires discipline and self-examination while they wait. Yet it is in these situations that light comes, because light shines in the darkness, where it is least understood.

If you've read through this book and your wait is up, then I am happy for you. It won't be long until there is a new wait, a new place that God will shine upon on your behalf. More than likely, however, your wait is probably not yet up just because you've concluded this book. Go back and start it again if you need or take what you've read and embrace the principles. As you wait through your dark period, learn about patience. Learn self-discipline in a new way. See God reach out to you in a million little ways through small glimmers of hope. Let the light shine in your life; first in little ways, and then in bigger ones.

Remember, light always shines in the darkness. If you want to see the light, you must first acknowledge and experience the darkness.

– REFERENCES –

<u>Epigraph</u>:

Dr. Seuss. "The Waiting Place." *Oh, the Places You'll Go!*. New York: Random House Books for Young Readers, 1960.

– Other Books of Interest by the Author –

- *A Heart God Can Use: The Journey to the Center of His Will* (Remnant Words, 2018)

- *All I Know About Ministry…I Learned in Junior High* (Righteous Pen Publications, 2017)

- *Between the Porch and the Altar: A Journey Through the Book of Joel* (Righteous Pen Publications, 2016, 2024)

- *Created for Love: An Evolution of Love in the Bible (And What it Means for Us)* (Remnant Words, 2019)

- *Manifestations of the Spirit: The Work of the Holy Spirit in the Church and in Your Life* (Righteous Pen Publications, 2019)

- *Power for Today: Practical Spirituality for Everyday Living (Volume 1)* (Righteous Pen Publications, 2016)

- *Seeds for the Season: 91 Days of Breakthrough* (Righteous Pen Publications, 2018)

– ABOUT THE AUTHOR –

NOR WILL PEOPLE SAY, LOOK! HERE [IT IS]! OR, SEE, [IT IS] THERE! FOR BEHOLD, THE KINGDOM OF GOD IS WITHIN YOU [IN YOUR HEARTS] AND AMONG YOU [SURROUNDING YOU].
(LUKE 17:21)

Dr. Lee Ann B. Marino, Ph.D., D.Min., D.D. (she/her) is "everyone's favorite theologian" leading Gen X, Millennials, and Gen Z with expertise in leadership training, queer and feminist theology, general religion, and apostolic theology. She has served in ministry since 1998 and was ordained as a pastor in 2002 and an apostle in 2010. She founded what is now Sanctuary Apostolic Fellowship Empowerment (SAFE) Ministries in 2004. Under her ministry heading Dr. Marino is founder and Overseer of Sanctuary International Fellowship Tabernacle (SIFT) (the original home of National Coming Out Sunday) and The Sanctuary Network, and Chancellor of Apostolic Covenant Theological Seminary (ACTS).

Affectionately nicknamed "the Spitfire," Dr. Marino has spent over two decades as an "apostle, preacher, and teacher" (2 Timothy 1:11), exercising her personal mandate to become "all things to all people" (1 Corinthians 9:22). Her embrace of spiritual issues (both technical and intimate) has found its home among both seekers and believers, those who desire spiritual answers to today's issues.

Dr. Marino has preached throughout the United States, Puerto Rico, and Europe in hundreds of religious services and experiences throughout the years. A history maker in her own right, she has spent over two decades in advocacy, education, and work for and within minority spiritual communities (including African American, Hispanic, and LGBTQ+). She has also served as the first woman on all-male synods, councils, and panels, as well as the first preacher or speaker welcomed of a different race, sexual orientation, or identity among diverse communities. Today, Dr. Marino's work extends to over 150 countries as she hosts the popular *Kingdom Now* podcast, which is in the top 20 percentile of all podcasts worldwide. She is also the author of over 35 books and the popular Patheos column, *Leadership on Fire*. To date, she has had five bestselling titles within their subject matter: *Understanding Demonology, Spiritual Warfare, Healing, and Deliverance: A Manual for the Christian Minister*; *Ministry School Boot Camp: Training for Helps Ministries, Appointments, and Beyond*; *Discovering Intimacy: A Journey Through the Song of Solomon*; *Fruit of the Vine: Study and Commentary on the Fruit of the Spirit*; and *Ministering to LGBTQ+ (and Those Who Love Them): A Primer for Queer Theology* (and its accompanying workbook).

As a public icon and social media influencer, Dr. Marino advocates healthy body image (curvy/full-figured), representation as a demisexual/aromantic, and albinism awareness as a model. Known to those she works with, she is a spiritual mom, teacher, leader, professor, confidant, and friend. She continues to transform, receiving new teaching, revelation, and insight in this thing we call "ministry." Through years of spiritual growth and maturity, Dr. Marino stands as herself, here to present what God has given to her for any who have an ear to hear.

For more information, visit her website at kingdompowernow.org.

www.ingramcontent.com/pod-product-compliance
Lightning Source LLC
Chambersburg PA
CBHW071411040426
42444CB00009B/2203